ISSUES IN OUR WORLD
GENETIC REVOLUTION

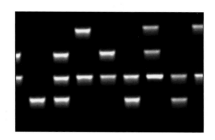

Ewan McLeish

Aladdin / Watts
London • Sydney

ABOUT THIS BOOK

Since the discovery of the genetic code in the 1950s, scientists have begun to unlock the secrets of life. We even have the power to create exact copies of ourselves. This book explores this genetic revolution, how it works and the effects it may have on our life.

© Aladdin Books Ltd 2009

Designed and produced by Aladdin Books Ltd
PO Box 53987
London SW15 2SF

ISBN 978 0 7496 8629 1

First published in 2009
by Franklin Watts
338 Euston Road
London NW1 3BH

Franklin Watts Australia
Level 17/207 Kent Street
Sydney NSW 2000

Franklin Watts is a division of Hachette Children's Books,
an Hachette Livre UK company.
www.hachettelivre.co.uk

A CIP record for this book is available from the British
Library

Dewey Classification: 660.6'5

Printed in Malaysia

Designer: Flick, Book Design and Graphics
Editor: Harriet Brown, Vivian Foster
Picture Research: Alexa Brown
The author: Dr. Ewan McLeish is a writer and lecturer in
education. He has written over 20 books on science and
the environment.
The consultant: Dr. Jon Turney is a senior visiting fellow
in the Department of Science and Technology Studies,
University College London, and a visiting lecturer in the
Science Communication Group at Imperial College,
London, UK.

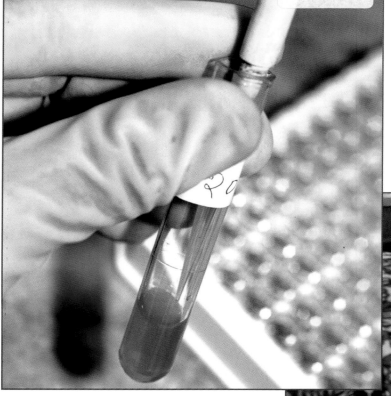

CONTENTS

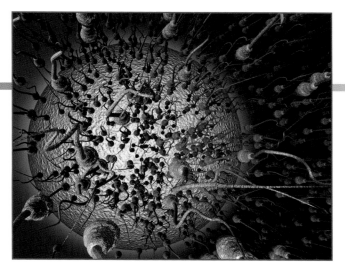

INTRODUCTION

Have you ever wondered how we come to look the way we do or why a seed grows into a particular plant? The answer lies in genes. All living organisms have a genetic code which dictates how they will develop. This code determines the colour of your hair or the shape of a leaf. Today it is possible to change the genetic code, but do you think this is a good thing or bad?

Boy in a bubble

Richard has spent his whole life in a plastic bubble, and without it he would die. Richard has no defence against germs because of a problem with his genetic code. Until a cure is found the best way to keep Richard alive is to keep him away from bacteria and viruses and this is why he lives in a bubble.

Cotton capers

In India, cotton is very important as it provides their main income. The bollworm (a small caterpillar) loves to eat cotton and the only way to get rid of it is with harmful chemicals. The problem is that these chemicals kill the good bugs as well, and pollute the rivers and streams.

Bollworms destroy cotton plants.

The power of life

The genetic revolution may also bring dangers. This technology is very powerful and as yet we do not know what effect it will have on us and our world. Some people believe we should continue to experiment, while others think we should not rush into the new genetic age.

Two problems – one solution?

Two very different problems, but they may have a common solution – to change the genetic codes. If Richard's genes were changed it might help him develop the healthy white blood cells he needs to fight infection. If the cotton plant had different genes it might be able to fight off the bollworm itself.

Start of a revolution

We are now able to take the gene from one organism, say a goldfish, and put it in a strawberry so that it can grow in cold conditions. We have the power to make exact copies of farm animals. We can make life-saving drugs by using human genes. We are now at the start of a genetic revolution.

SOME HELPFUL TERMS
Bases – The parts of the DNA molecule that determine the genetic code.
Cells – The tiny building blocks from which all organisms are made.
Chromosome – A long strand of DNA.
DNA – A molecule in the shape of a spiral staircase. DNA is found inside cells.
Gene – A short section of DNA. Genes tell the body how to develop and determine which characteristics are passed on to the next generation.
Genetic code – The set of instructions that determines the growth, type, shape and other characteristics of a living organism.
Genetic engineering – The alteration of the genetic code of an organism.
GM – Genetic modification, or genetically modified.

5

GENES 'R' US

In the middle of the 20th century scientists made an important discovery. They were about to tell the world about a substance in cells they knew to be at the heart of the genetic code – the substance was called DNA. No one realised at the time quite how important this discovery was.

DNA revealed

The discovery of DNA's structure by two scientists helped to explain how every plant and animal comes to look the way it does. Even more importantly, it gave a clue to how this information was passed from generation to generation. In 1953, the scientists were studying a molecule called DNA that they knew played a vital role in controlling features such as your height or hair and eye colour. They found the molecule's shape

Watson and Crick discovered the double helix shape of DNA. This unlocked the sequence of the genetic code.

was a spiral made of two long strands, joined by shorter cross-strands, very similar to a twisted rope ladder. This became known as the famous double helix.

The two scientists were Francis Crick from Britain and James Watson from America. Overnight they became the most famous scientists in the world.

DNA – the stuff of life

Organisms are made from tiny cells which form our tissues and organs. At the centre of each cell is the nucleus. Inside the nucleus are X-shaped chromosomes. Each living thing has a different number of chromosomes – humans have 46 per cell. Half of the chromosomes come from the mother and half from the father.

Chromosomes are made of tightly coiled DNA and on each chromosome are many genes. As you can see, DNA really is the stuff of life.

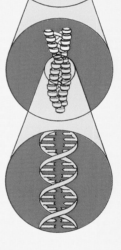

Each cell contains a nucleus.

Chromosomes are found inside the nucleus.

Chromosomes are packages of tightly coiled DNA.

Each gene is a section of the DNA spiral.

Genes describe the formation of the body, how it looks and how it functions.

7

Each rung is made from two chemicals called bases. The arrangement of the bases forms a code.

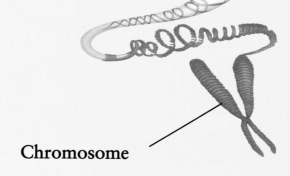

In this diagram, each different colour – green, blue, pink and orange – is a different base. There are only four bases in total.

Chromosome

All about genes

Watson and Crick's brilliant discovery was that genes are actually segments of DNA. The illustration on the previous page explains how the DNA's 'ladder' is made up of rungs called 'bases'. The order in which the bases are arranged on the DNA strand forms the code by which genetic messages can be created. Each new message is a different gene.

Proteins = life

Each gene tells the cell to produce a molecule on which all life is based – a protein. We all need proteins to grow and develop. For our bodies to work properly, thousands of chemical reactions are taking place in our cells. These reactions cannot take place without the help of proteins. Proteins are made from smaller building blocks called amino acids. Our genes tell the cell how to put these blocks together so that our bodies receive the essential proteins.

When genes go wrong

Sometimes genes do not work perfectly and a fault develops in the DNA's code. This means our body does not produce the essential proteins, which can then result in a crippling illness like cystic fibrosis. Most of the time, however, our genes do work perfectly.

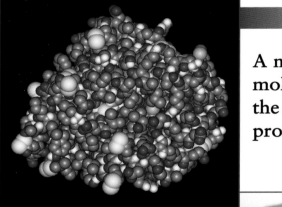

A model of a protein molecule. Genes tell the body which proteins to create.

8

Genetic modification

In 1983, exactly 30 years after the structure of DNA was discovered, scientists made another major breakthrough. They managed to transfer a gene from a microscopic organism – a bacterium – into a tobacco plant. This was the first time a plant had been genetically modified.

Today, you have probably heard the term 'genetic modification' (GM) on the news. GM started to appear in the food we eat and the subject raised strong emotions both for and against.

Much debate surrounds the growing and eating of genetically modified crops.

Genetic modification plays an important role from medicine to manufacturing, from farming to forensics. Imagine you can remove faulty genes and replace them with ones that work. This discovery gives us the power to change life. The next chapter shows the many ways of transferring genes from one organism to another, allowing us to modify almost any living thing.

9

Tobacco was one of the first plants to be genetically modified.

TRANSFERRING GENES

Moving genes from one organism to another is not a simple process and often ends in failure. Genes are often moved by using 'carriers' such as a bacterium. People who suffer from diabetes have benefited from this process.

Many diabetics must have insulin injections every day.

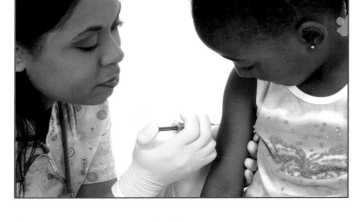

WHAT IS DIABETES?

Close to the small intestine is a large organ called the pancreas. In healthy people the pancreas produces insulin, which converts glucose in the blood. In diabetics, the pancreas does not work properly. Without the right amount of insulin, their blood glucose levels rise and they become very sick. In most cases, diabetes can be controlled by taking insulin at regular intervals.

Where to find insulin?

Insulin once came from animals such as pigs and cows, but when an outbreak of 'mad cow disease' occurred in 1986, scientists needed to find an alternative source. What they needed was a large supply of insulin that could be produced quickly and to the same high quality every time.

Supplies of insulin used to come from pigs or cows.

Bacteria to the rescue

The answer to the problem came in the form of a bacterium called *Escherichia coli (E. coli* for short). This was a common bacterium that scientists were familiar with and that was easy to grow in a laboratory. The gene that produces insulin in humans was inserted into the genetic code of the bacteria, and after many years of research the supply of insulin was no longer a problem.

Plasmids do the work

Bacteria have extra genetic material called plasmids. A plasmid is a tiny piece of DNA which can be taken out of the bacterium and modified before being put back.

E. coli is a bacteria commonly used in scientific research.

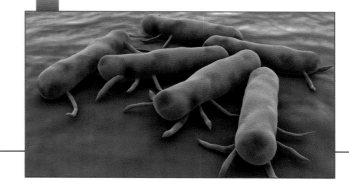

 ## How is this done?

First, cells are taken from the pancreas of a healthy person using special chemicals called enzymes.

• These chemicals are used to cut out a piece of bacterial DNA (plasmid), leaving a gap for the insulin gene.
• The insulin gene is then inserted into the plasmid.
• Other chemicals are used to seal the join.
• The plasmid is returned to the bacterium which now contains the insulin gene.

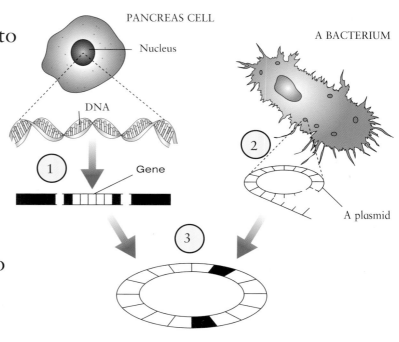

11

The bacterium now carries the insulin-producing gene. Bacteria reproduce by dividing repeatedly so that soon there are millions of exact copies of the original bacterium. Each of these new bacteria will be capable of producing human insulin.

TARGET PRACTICE

Using plasmids is not the only way of putting a new gene into another organism. In genetically modified plants, genes can be shot into the cell's nucleus by attaching them to tiny particles of gold or tungsten metal.

Viruses are microscopic organisms that are capable of causing diseases such as measles or the common cold. Viruses can also invade cells. Once inside they mix their own DNA with that of the animal or human they have invaded. The virus then makes the host's cells produce thousands of copies of itself. Eventually there are so many viruses in the cell that they break out and go on to infect other cells.

Safety first

Because viruses are so clever at combining their own DNA with that of their host, it makes them ideal carriers for genes. Genes can be inserted into the virus and the modified virus is put into the host. Because a virus can carry disease it needs to be made safe so that it does not make more copies of itself.

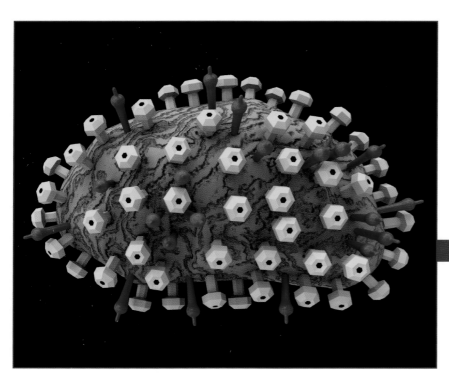

Viruses can be used to transfer genes into an organism.

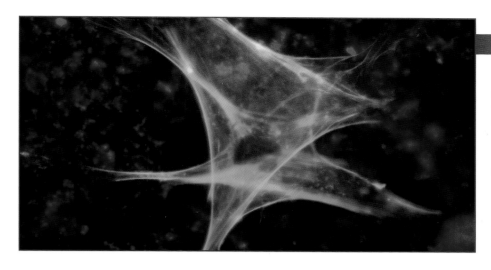

Liposomes fuse with the cell membrane (*green area*) that surrounds the cell.

For this reason the use of viruses in genetic modification does carry risks.

Luckily other mechanisms are available, for example, liposomes. Liposomes are minute oil-like droplets found inside cells, that can merge with the membrane that surrounds all animal cells. In this way they can carry genes into the cell.

NOTHING NEW?

We have used biotechnology for thousands of years. For example, plants and animals have been specially bred to make them more resistant to disease. Another example is the making of bread, wine and beer which uses a microscopic fungus called yeast.

It was the discovery of the genetic code by Watson and Crick in 1953 that led to the advancement of moving genes from one organism to another. Today, genetic modification is part of our daily lives, even if many people are not aware of it.

13

The Roman way

Ninety per cent of copper mined today is 'biomined', or using bacteria to extract the mineral. The largest mine is the Quebrada Blanca in Chile.

Reels of copper wire

GM CROPS

One of the more common uses of genetic engineering is in genetically modified (GM) food. Is it safe to eat? Does it harm the environment? Here we look at some facts regarding GM food so you can make up your own mind.

There has been much talk about giant or strangely-shaped GM foods, such as fruit and vegetables.

WHAT'S IN A NAME?
The term 'genetically modified' can mean many different things. Look at the box on the opposite page for more details.

The unsquashable tomato
The first GM food to be produced commercially appeared in American supermarkets in 1994. It was a tomato that was modified to stay firmer for longer. This meant not only was it easier to transport but it had a longer shelf life. Since then many other GM products have made their way onto our plates.

Benefits of GM crops
Crops are modified in a variety of ways. By changing the plant's genetic code, it can be made resistant to herbicides or pesticides and more hardy so that it can grow in poor soil. GM crops have been beneficial to farmers and consumers all over the world. This is especially true in the developing world where food is scarce. Despite the many benefits, people are still suspicious.

14

Guide to GM food

GM food – Food coming directly from a crop or animal that has been genetically modified.

GM ingredients – Food containing a GM product, such as GM maize flour.

GM processing aid – Food in which a GM organism has been used to produce a product, such as cheese making.

GM derived ingredients – Food that comes from a GM crop but no longer contains GM DNA, for example, soy oil.

GM ingredients in animal feed – Refers to the meat that comes from animals fed on GM crops.

There is no evidence that eating GM foods can make you ill.

So what's all the fuss about GM products?

Is GM food safe to eat?

The main concern people have regarding GM food, is whether it is safe to eat. The idea of 'foreign' genes being inserted into plants and animals causes concern regarding people's health.

The other concern is the 'antibiotic resistance'. Because antibiotics are sometimes used to find and select cells, some people feel that antibiotic-resistant cells may be passed on to humans and make them immune to vital medicines.

Exaggerated concerns

Other people feel that these concerns are grossly exaggerated. All food products are tested before being sold, which includes checking for harmful products.

At present, there is little evidence to suggest that eating GM foods can be harmful. The question of antibiotic resistance is more difficult to answer. There is some evidence that harmless bacteria in the gut can take up antibiotic resistance from GM products. There is, however, no evidence that this can be transferred to other cells in the body, or to other harmful organisms.

15

The case of the genetically modified soya

In April 2003, a toxic cloud formed over Colonia Loma Senés, in Argentina. The cloud contained poisonous droplets which made the villagers' eyes sting and the children's bare legs develop nasty rashes. All the crops in the region were badly damaged, chickens and pigs died and goats gave birth to dead or deformed young. The villagers blamed neighbouring farmers who were growing GM soya on their land.

What had happened?

The soya had been modified to make it resistant to a very strong herbicide called glyphosphate. The herbicide was meant to kill the weeds and not the soya.

Herbicide spraying has increased as a result of growing GM soya.

At first the results were promising, and soon almost half the land was used for soya. Gradually things started to go wrong. The farmers had to use more herbicides as the weeds became resistant, and the beneficial soil bacteria started to decline. Yields began to fail.

Gain or blame?

Most people blamed the GM soya. Over 150,000 farmers were driven from their land and the production of staples like milk, rice, maize, potatoes and lentils fell sharply. With proper supervision, perhaps such problems would not have arisen.

People blamed GM soya for their problems as it required powerful herbicides not normally used.

DO GM CROPS HARM THE ENVIRONMENT?

Even if GM crops are safe to eat, there are still other concerns. Plants that have been genetically modified should require less harmful herbicides, but this is not always the case. There is also the concern that GM crops could harm beneficial insects and the birds that feed on them.

Contamination is also a worry. What if some of the genes inserted into the crops 'escaped' and got into weeds? Might we be creating 'super-weeds'?

Although evidence is far from clear, a survey carried out in the UK between 1999 and 2003 found that some fields containing GM crops contained fewer bees and butterflies than normal crops.

On the plus side, though, the worldwide growth of GM crops is helping to reduce the effect of harmful greenhouse gas emissions from farm machinery.

Some GM crops have proved to be good for wildlife, while others caused a reduction in numbers.

17

Some people campaign against GM foods, while others support it.

More research needed?

Trials are being carried out to see what long term effects GM crops will have on our environment. These trials, however, have caused many arguments. The difficulty comes in deciding whether the benefits, such as providing enough food for people, using less chemicals and reducing greenhouse emissions, outweigh the possible dangers.

ANIMAL FARM

So far we have only looked at genetically modified crops, but what about animals? Research is being carried out to create cows that produce richer milk and sheep with softer wool. In Japan, a scientist even created a pig implanted with a spinach gene to try and make it healthier to eat.

Right or wrong?

How do you feel about these experiments with animals? Unlike plants, animals are aware of what is going on around them. They feel pain and discomfort and, as such, should be treated with respect. Is it morally wrong to try and genetically modify an animal purely for our own benefit?

18

Some people say it is no different to the way we have been farming for thousands of years. For example, animals have been bred to have certain characteristics by repeatedly mating only those with the desired features. Eventually, the gene for high milk production becomes established in their young. This is called selective breeding.

Is this selective breeding really any different from modifying an animal's genes in a laboratory? Many people feel that as long as the animal does not suffer in any way, then genetic modification is a beneficial advancement in science.

In the name of the law?

In European countries, it is legal to grow or import GM food products, as long as the risks to our health and the environment have been carefully monitored. Many of these imports come from the US and Canada. This also applies to the rearing and welfare of animals.

Despite these restrictions, there are still plenty of GM products imported into Europe from countries that are not so strict. As we have seen, countries like Argentina grow a large amount of GM soya every year, much of which ends up in cattle feed. People in other countries may then eat the meat from these GM-soya-fed cattle.

Many cattle are now fed on genetically modified soya.

In some countries, food labels tell you whether the product contains any GM foods. Other countries, like the US and Canada, are not so strict.

WHAT'S IN YOUR SHOPPING BASKET?

Although eating GM foods does not seem to cause harm to health, some people still have their doubts. Many supermarkets have decided to ban GM ingredients in their own brands, but are unable to guarantee that meat is reared on a GM-free diet unless it is marked 'organic'.

This is where labelling comes in. In 2004, new EU regulations were agreed, designed to give customers more information about what they are eating. Any product containing any GM ingredients or produced from GM crops, had to be included on the label. Other parts of the world quickly followed.

Problems with labelling

Of course it is not easy to track all the ingredients and many people feel that the labelling is not accurate. This is particularly true of cheeses made using GM bacteria or animals raised on GM feed. In most countries, however, food in our supermarkets is safe for human consumption.

FEED THE WORLD?

Many people all over the world suffer because they do not have enough to eat. Genetic engineering could possibly solve some of the world's food shortages by creating crops that thrive in harsh conditions.

TOUGH PLANTS

In 2004, a group of scientists produced some revolutionary plants. Using genetic engineering, these scientists created tomato and rice plants that would survive harsh conditions. Rather than adding genes from other plants, they increased the plants' own natural defences by boosting their own genes. One of these clever genes made the plant pump salt out of its roots, before the salt in the soil could do any damage. In many poorer parts of the world, many plants die because there is too much salt in the soil. This means many previously infertile areas could be brought back into production.

Many crops die because of poor soil conditions or lack of rainfall.

Something for nothing?

Many people believe this could make the soil problem worse. They argue it would be better to use irrigation to improve the salt levels in the first place.

The advantage of this type of genetic engineering means that they do not have to introduce genes from other animals or plants. Only time will tell how successful this method really is.

crippling the population, we hear of success stories. For example, the gene that made cotton plants resistant to the invasive bollworm then killed any bollworms that ate the plants.

Planting GM cotton has increased yields by making it resistant to the bollworm.

MORE TOUGH CHOICES?

People still argue whether we have the right to mix genes between species and what overall effect it will have on our environment. This is a particularly tough decision when it comes to helping countries where food is scarce. Where chronic malnutrition and poverty are

This new cotton plant was called 'Bt'. Supporters claim that Bt allowed farmers to use less pesticides, and that it increased the cotton yield by between 30 and 80 per cent. Added to this, it was more environmentally friendly because the pesticide they did use only killed moth and butterfly caterpillars.

Read what people have to say:

People in the rich countries can protest against using GM all they like. They can afford not to use the technology. We don't have the choice!

KIRAN SHARMA, SCIENTIST AT THE INTERNATIONAL CROPS RESEARCH INSTITUTE FOR THE SEMI-ARID TROPICS, INDIA.

The (GM) companies have nothing to offer the poor . . . Why gamble on a potentially dangerous technology with economic risks, when old fashioned selective breeding has served so well?

SUMAN SAHAI, ORGANISER OF AN ANTI-GM GROUP, INDIA.

Spanning the world

Cotton is not the only crop to get the GM treatment, and it is happening all over the world. Recent developments include a type of rice that has been made to produce high levels of a chemical called beta-carotene. The human body needs beta-carotene to produce vitamin A. Without this vitamin people would go blind.

In developing countries blindness is a major problem, and it is hoped that this new variety of rice will help prevent this condition.

23

Is it possible that genetically modified rice could help improve people's eyesight?

GM companies – the answer or the problem?

Some people believe that the biotechnology companies have forced GM products onto poor farmers. The worry is that the companies concerned have invested so much money into these projects, that they need to find a way to get their money back.

Some people also believe that GM technology is threatening the traditional ways of producing food. They argue that the real cause of world hunger is not the lack of food, but poverty. They say that the world should address this issue and not put money into the pockets of the large biotechnology companies.

The way ahead?

ICRISAT is a public-funded research institute and its director general says:

We see ourselves as the acceptable face of GM, since we are trying to ensure the products we are developing will benefit the poor in the semi-arid tropics.

We need to look at both sides of the argument and weigh them up. Perhaps now is the time to make way for both old and new technologies and let developing countries decide for themselves.

Some people believe that GM technology will harm traditional ways of producing food.

24

'PHARMING' TO FABRICS

We have seen how bacteria can be modified to produce insulin, but now let us look at other genetically made medicines. Plants can also be modified to produce drugs and this new cultivation is called 'pharming'.

Scientists have made artificial spider silk protein in goat's milk, creating strands stronger than steel.

Help for haemophiliacs

Haemophilia is a disease in which the blood does not clot. If a blood vessel is damaged, a scab will not form and it will bleed for a very long time. This is because a haemophiliac lacks the blood-clotting agent called Factor VIII, found in healthy blood. Genetic engineering has allowed scientists to make Factor VIII in the laboratory, with the added bonus of being totally free of viruses.

Stronger than steel

A biotechnology company in Canada developed artificial spider silk for use in making artificial tendons and ligaments. These are the structures that hold muscles onto bones and support the skeleton. The silk-producing genes are cultivated in goat's milk and the resultant proteins can be turned into Bio Steel.

Combating lung disease

In 1993, scientists produced a genetically modified sheep that could supply medicines for people with the lung disease emphysema. They gave the sheep the name Tracey and she was modified with human genes. Tracey produced milk containing large quantities of human alpha-1-antitrypsin (AAT). Just imagine how much AAT one thousand Traceys could produce.

Sheep's milk can be used to make genetically modified products.

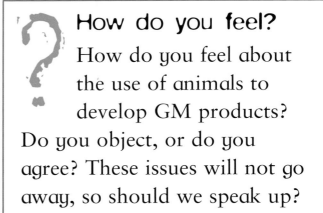

How do you feel?
How do you feel about the use of animals to develop GM products? Do you object, or do you agree? These issues will not go away, so should we speak up?

goldfish that glows in a certain type of light. The genetic revolution is gathering pace day by day and assists in saving and improving the health of many people. So why are people so worried about it?

The main problem is contamination. In one case, a GM tomato was inserted with a virus that caused severe digestive problems. Scientists in Arizona had hoped to use the tomato to make a vaccine to the illness. They have solved the contamination problem by using an easily identified white tomato!

GM gathers pace

Today the list of genetically modified organisms (GMOs) is almost endless. Soon we may be able to buy designer pets, such as a

Scientists have put virus genes into white tomatoes.

GENE THERAPY

In 2003, scientists discovered the sequences of 'letters' that make up the human genome (the entire human genetic code). It was called the Human Genome Project. It opened up the possibility of fixing faulty genes.

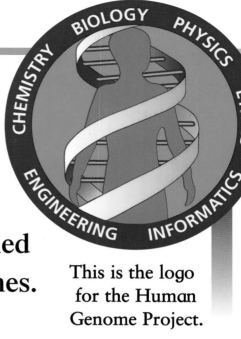

This is the logo for the Human Genome Project.

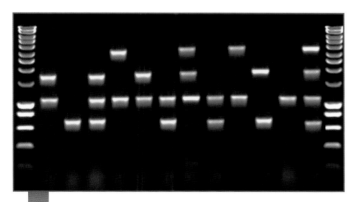

Scientists can analyse DNA samples to identify genes that cause disease.

Genome

The Human Genome Project was started in 1995. It had the support of many governments, charities and pharmaceutical companies from all over the world. By the end of 1999, the genetic code for one complete human chromosome was known. By 2001, nearly 95 per cent of the genome in humans had been discovered, and a kind of 'rough draft' was produced.

Their final goal was reached just two years later, when around 25,000 genes had been identified, made up from over 3 billion bases. Surprisingly, only 3 per cent of these bases actually formed the genes themselves.

The gene repair shop

Mapping the entire human genome was an amazing feat. By understanding more about our genes, it is now possible to identify the faulty gene that causes the problem. Perhaps, in the future, this knowledge will enable us to cure genetic disease.

Gene therapy

Repairing faulty genes in humans – gene therapy – is a difficult task. The are many risks and the price of failure is high.

Plan of action

On page 4 we talked about the boy who had to live in a bubble. He had a condition called Severe Combined Immune Deficiency (SCID). One way to save a SCID patient is to give them a bone marrow transplant. However, to do this you need to find a suitable donor, and finding a perfect match is difficult.

SCID is caused by a faulty gene. This gene is normally responsible for producing an enzyme called adenosine deaminase (ADA). ADA is necessary for white blood cells, or T-cells, to function normally. In healthy people, the T-cells recognise faulty cells that have been infected by a virus and destroy the contaminated cell.

28

How is gene therapy used to treat SCID?

• Bone marrow cells are taken from the patient.
• An ADA gene from a healthy donor is inserted into a virus.
• The virus is used to transfer the gene into the patient's bone marrow cells.
• Modified bone marrow cells are put back into the patient.

Sadly, gene therapy in SCID sufferers has caused cancer in some patients.

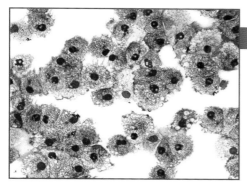

Patients with SCID have faulty white blood cells.

Using gene therapy on SCID patients is risky and sometimes there are nasty side effects. In a couple of patients, they developed a cancer called leukaemia, in which blood cells start multiplying out of control. The virus that was used to deliver the gene activated another gene, which triggered the cancer. Because of this side effect, the trials for gene therapy for replacing ADA genes were put on hold.

'Fingers' to the rescue?

In April 2005, scientists in the US announced they had found another way of delivering the gene without the use of a virus. They used a chemical 'finger'. The finger was made up of building blocks of proteins (amino acids) attached to a zinc atom. This chemical finger recognises where the faulty gene lies, cuts open the DNA, and allows the normal gene to be inserted. So far this revolutionary technique has had very encouraging results.

Genetic therapy promises cures for many different genetic diseases.

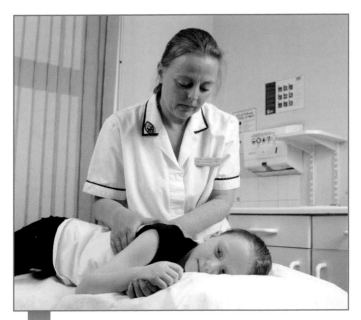

Cystic fibrosis patients must have regular physiotherapy to help them breathe.

Cystic fibrosis

Cystic fibrosis is a common genetic disorder. In the UK, over 7,500 people suffer from the disease. In this disease too much water is lost from the air passages and they become clogged with sticky mucus. Patients find it hard to breathe and their lungs are unable to fight off bacteria.

Gene therapy for cystic fibrosis

Like SCID, cystic fibrosis is caused by a faulty gene. At first the only gene therapy available involved spraying the air passages

with a genetically modified virus. This process is difficult as the air passages are so narrow.

In 2004, scientists came up with a new approach – using the patient's stem cells to deliver the gene. Adult stem cells are made in the bone marrow. Because they are unspecialised cells they are able to develop into any other type of cell in the body, for example, the type of cell that can line the air passages. The advantage of this type of gene therapy is that stem cells are not attacked by the patient's immune system.

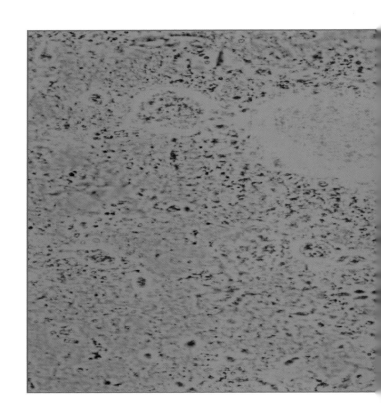

What about the benefits?

The benefits of gene therapy could be enormous. Do we have the right to deny patients treatment that could cure previously incurable diseases? Would you be prepared to undergo gene therapy if you had the chance?

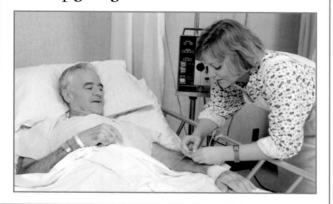

This is because they come from the patient's own body. In the future it is hoped that this method could provide a more permanent solution for such a crippling disease.

Too far, too fast?

Because gene therapy is such a new science, it raises many difficult issues. Many people are concerned that the viruses used could be dangerous, especially if they are taken from animals. We have seen that there can be unpredicable effects, such as the triggering of cancers. As gene 'delivery' advances, it is hoped that the problems associated with viruses will be overcome, and it will be possible to help more sufferers of genetic diseases.

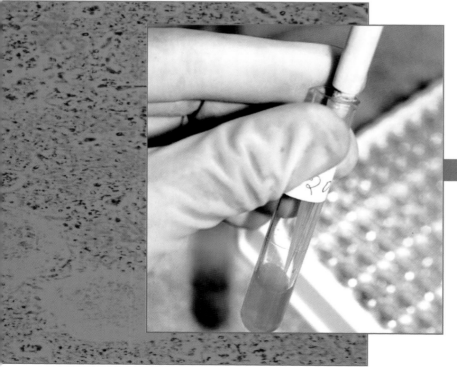

The left-hand image shows stem cells (the larger circles) under a microscope. Stem cell gene therapy may help to transform the lives of many people with genetic diseases.

Genetic Screening

Today, scientists can check embryos to find out whether they have any faulty genes. This is called genetic screening. It can be used to tell whether a person is likely to develop a genetic disease – for example, a rare genetic condition called FAP, which can lead to life-threatening bowel cancer in later life.

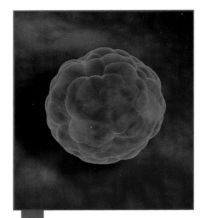

This is a blastocyst—an embryo at a very early stage.

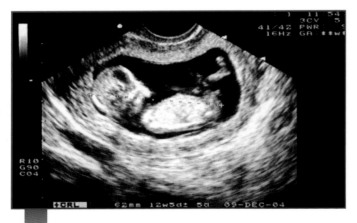

This is a scan of a 12-week-old foetus. Can you see the head?

A difference of opinion

The reason for choosing to scan for FAP is that families with the genetic condition have a 50 per cent chance of passing it on to their children. Those people against this type of genetic screening claim that 'we are not thinking about curing the disease but eliminating the carrier'.

Discarding embryos with the faulty gene would mean that this gene could gradually be eliminated.

What is IVF?

IVF or '*in vitro* fertilisation' is where eggs are fertilised outside of the womb. Cells are removed for analysis and, depending on the outcome, the healthy egg is put in the womb for a normal pregnancy.

Many people believe that this is a wonderful idea, while others feel it could have other more serious implications.

New science, old choices

The idea of genetic screening is not new. In the past, it was possible to look at several generations of families in which a genetic disorder occurred. From this, it was possible to work out if a couple were likely to have a child that would inherit the disease.

Today, many pregnant women undergo screening. If both parents carry a faulty gene – for example,

cystic fibrosis – and the embryo is found to be at risk of developing the disease, then they face the agonising decision of whether or not to end the pregnancy. It is now known that the gene in cystic fibrosis is very complex. Sometimes the disease will occur, sometimes not, making the decision even harder.

Decisions, decisions

The decision to destroy an embryo is not taken lightly. A child may not thank its parents for allowing it to be born with a handicap or disease that would cut short its life. On the other hand, life is precious and many people with handicaps go on to lead full and productive lives.

As genetic tests become more sophisticated, there will come a point where we will have to ask ourselves where we draw the line. What do we eliminate and what do we allow through the genetic net? This is a hard decision and one that will probably get harder.

33

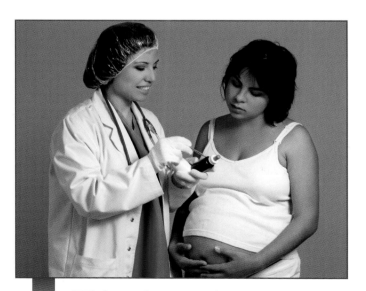

With an increase in genetic screening, couples are finding it harder to make decisions.

Saving siblings

In April 2005, a couple were legally allowed to screen and select embryos in order to produce a genetic match for an older brother. The boy had a severe blood disorder called beta-thalassemia. He needed regular blood transfusions to stay alive. Stem cells from the younger child could save his life and allow him to make his own healthy red blood cells.

Babies on demand?

Many people objected to what they called a 'designer' baby. They claimed it was wrong to create a 'special' baby, even if it was for the benefit of others. The question here is – where to draw the line? Would it be right to design your own child – for example, to choose its sex, colour of hair or perhaps one of higher intelligence?

Changing genes in eggs and sperm

In gene therapy, normal genes are inserted into cells to replace faulty ones. There is no way that these modified genes can be passed on. However, scientists also have the ability to modify genes in the sex cells or the eggs and sperm. This is known as germ line gene therapy and is banned almost everywhere in the world.

This does not involve changing the genetic make-up of just one human being. Eggs and sperm can pass on their genes to the next generation!

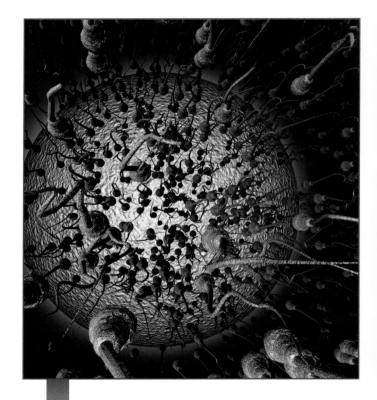

A sperm cell penetrates the egg cell during fertilisation to create an embryo.

CLONING & STEM CELLS

Normally, a person is created when two cells – a male and a female sex cell – join together. A clone is created from one ordinary cell – not a sex cell – and is genetically identical to its one and only parent. So cloning is an identical copy of an original.

Embryonic stem cells could be used to create new tissues.

How was it done?

The first human embryo was cloned in the UK in May 2005. It was done by taking a donated human egg cell and removing its genetic material (the nucleus). A skin cell was taken from the patient and the nucleus from this cell was injected into the donor egg cell. The egg cell began to divide forming an early human embryo which was genetically identical to the patient.

Stem cells from clones

The cloned embryos could be used as a source of embryonic stem cells. Stem cells are 'master' cells that can develop into any tissue in the body. These cells could be used to cure their own diseases or even create new organs, without fear of rejection by the body's immune system.

Identical twins are genetically the same, that is, they are clones of each other.

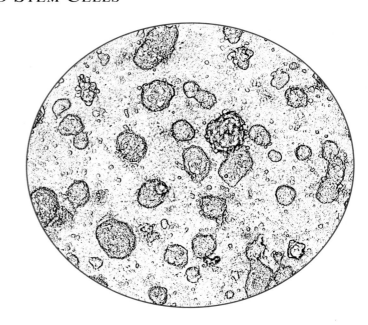

Benefits of stem cell therapy

Curing ailments such as Parkinson's disease has now become a possibility. In this case, stem cells from an embryo, cloned from the patient, might replace dead nerve cells in the brain. Cloned cells could also help in the study of the diseases as well.

The pendulum swings

Many people are appalled at the use of human embryos in this way. They worry that this is the first step to producing a fully developed cloned baby. Without knowing what all the dangers might be in cloning, some fear that cells that are genetically identical could introduce harmful genes into hundreds of patients. It is important that we understand what is involved and distinguish between therapeutic and reproductive cloning.

Therapeutic cloning

Therapeutic cloning involves developing cloned embryos so that their stem cells (*above*) can be removed and used in research.

Reproductive cloning

This involves the cloning of a human being to produce a fully developed, genetically exact copy of that person. As far as we know, this has never been done. Reproductive cloning is currently banned internationally.

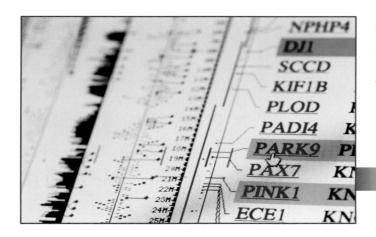

Embryonic stem cells could help to cure Parkinson's disease.

THE FUTURE

Research into finding new cures or treatments are advancing day by day, and soon we could use gene therapy to cure things such as blindness, deafness, cancer and brain diseases. Could genetic engineering one day prevent thousands of unnecessary deaths each year?

A healthy future?

In 2005, American scientists announced they had used gene therapy to cure deafness in guinea pigs. This research raised hopes that the same technique could be used on humans. In embryos there is a gene that controls the growth of inner ear hair cells, which often get damaged, say from loud noise or just old age. When this gene was inserted into the ear of a guinea pig, it helped generate new hair cells and restored its hearing by up to 80 per cent.

In the future, gene therapy could cure some forms of deafness.

More GM treatments

Scientists are now looking at the possibility of using adult stem cells to tackle liver disease. They want to take stem cells from the patient's bone marrow and then introduce them into the liver. It is hoped that the stem cells will start to act like liver cells and help the liver to repair itself.

In the future it may be possible to treat infectious diseases like tuberculosis (TB) with vaccines that are made of genetically engineered DNA. TB is caused by a bacterium. By modifying a segment of DNA, so that it contained genes from the bacterium, an individual could build up their own antibodies and become immune to the TB strain.

Could children soon have 47 chromosomes instead of 46?

A new treatment for AIDS?

A major breakthrough would be to use genetic modification against the deadly HIV virus – AIDS. It is a widespread problem in many parts of the world and in many cases is fatal, despite modern drugs.

Scientists know that the rhesus monkey has a gene that attacks the HIV virus. Humans have a different version of the same gene. Scientists hope to genetically modify this gene so that it reacts in the same way as those in the monkey. This may create a cure for AIDS.

More and more

There are plans to create artificial chromosomes as a way of delivering many different genes at the same time. Some scientists see this as the most promising form of gene therapy. Maybe children in the future will have an extra chromosome – 47 instead of 46!

Eugenics – the solution?

Eugenics is the deliberate attempt to change or modify entire populations. The Nazis tried to exterminate people they felt were inferior, in an effort to produce a pure or 'master' race. Their method was not genetic modification, but the killing of over 7 million people. In more

Gene therapy could one day be used to build muscle.

Designer world?

It is worrying that advancements in genetic engineering could have a more sinister side. A world without disease or disability would be great, but the rise of drugs to improve sporting performance is becoming a problem. Soon, it could be possible that gene therapy will be used to make muscles respond better to exercise. The research currently being carried out is aimed at treating muscular dystrophy, but the results have caught the attention of athletes.

Rights or wrongs?

The guinea pigs used in the experiment at the start of this chapter were first deafened by means of antibiotics. Almost all medical genetic work is carried out on animals, and to some people this is a major concern. Although there has been much success in the latest genetic engineering research, there have been the failures as well. Until scientists find out more, we will not know all the benefits.

recent times this has become known as 'ethnic cleansing'. Throughout history, societies have tried to rid themselves of groups who they felt were 'different', but have we learned from their actions?

In 1994 in Rwanda, ethnic cleansing killed between 500,000 and one million people. Could genetic engineering lead to a new kind of ethnic cleansing?

THE DEBATE

The following is part of a recent public debate called 'The Search for Perfection'. The group discussed whether it was right or wrong to modify embryos to eliminate unwanted features.

We should all involve ourselves in debates about genetic engineering.

John

John is a supporter of gene therapy and the modification of humans. He says: *'To choose to bring a child with diseases or disabilities into this world is morally a problem . . . If it is not wrong for a parent to wish to have a bonny, bouncing baby boy, how does it become wrong if we have the technology to grant our wish?'*

Tom

Tom has achondroplasia, which is an inherited disability causing restricted growth. He says: *'It is always interesting to listen to* John. Perhaps less so this time because the world he has in mind wouldn't have me in it. Or my two kids, or my dad . . . A good society looks after its weakest members regardless of disability or disease.'*

Kathy

Kathy is an editor of a fashion magazine and takes a completely different viewpoint. She says: *'Unlike Tom, you could say I don't live in the real world. But like it or not, cosmetic enhancement is part of the real world and there will always be a demand for these*

40

procedures . . . As soon as geneticists can tweak an embryo to produce a blonde, blue-eyed, long-limbed baby, there will be a customer. But the future population of Barbie dolls won't necessarily be content. In my experience, perfection often leads to more insecurity – and ultimately more surgery.'

Donald

Donald is a religious leader who says: *'We recently had a family in the US who were allowed to use IVF to choose an embryo of the same sex and as close a match as possible to their child who was*

suffering from a serious bone marrow disease. That same week, in another country, a family was turned down when they asked for IVF to select a girl to replace their only daughter lost in an accident . . . Is genetic engineering going to bring peace to the world? I don't think so.'

Each of the four people in our debate has a different viewpoint. Who do you agree with and who do you think is wrong?

Would you really want to live in a society where everyone is perfect?

The search for perfection

The debate highlights some complicated issues and choices. If we have children, most of us would want them to be healthy, strong and happy. But is that the same as being free from all medical conditions and disabilities? Is it right that we should hand pick a future child so that it can help its incurably sick brother or sister?

As this book shows, the genetic revolution goes much further than that. Perhaps there are really only two issues we need to consider. The first is why we want to intervene in this process; the second is what is the likely outcome?

The why question

This question will vary from person to person, and your answer will reflect your own values and background. What we find acceptable may not be acceptable to other people, and it is important that we respect these differences.

The what question

In some ways the question of 'what' is more difficult to answer. We cannot easily predict the consequences of our actions. When we change something, other things often change as a result.

We have seen evidence of this throughout this book. The question of human development involves an element of risk and our move into the genetic age is no exception.

To know or not to know?

Let us return to genetic screening. A medical team in Australia offered to screen 12,000 people for haemochromatosis, a condition which leads to liver and heart problems. The tests were accepted by 96 per cent of those offered it. Of those people scanned, 47 were identified as having the genetic defect, and all but one started having treatment. The study was considered to be a success.

Every human is wonderfully unique. Should we use our scientific knowledge to eliminate all genetic disease?

Not all conditions are this easy to detect, however. Tests for certain types of cancer can only give the patient an idea of the likelihood of contracting the disease. Knowledge of this risk could worry people, as well as helping them. We are faced with the difficult question – would we want to know if we had a potentially fatal disease, bearing in mind that an early warning could save lives?

No going back

It could be argued that there is no going back, and would we really want to even if we could? The genetic revolution may bring with it many responsibilities, but it also opens many doors which may be critical to our very future.

43

CHRONOLOGY

6000 BC – Sumerians make beer and wine by using a micro-organism, yeast.

2500 BC – Farmers in Egypt try an early example of selective breeding.

1719 – First hybrid plant created.

1869 – Frederick Miescher isolates DNA from cells for the first time.

1902 – Chromosomes are identified as the means by which characteristics are inherited.

1909 – Wilhelm Johannsen uses the word 'gene' for the first time for Mendel's 'unit' of inheritance.

1911 – Thomas Hunt Morgan studies fruit fly chromosomes and shows that they carry genes.

1943 – William Astbury reveals that DNA must have a regular, repeating structure.

1953 – Francis Crick and James Watson describe the double spiral (double helix) structure of DNA.

1955 – Joe Hin Tjio describes the exact number of chromosomes in human cells as 46.

1968 – Scientists identify the enzymes that recognise and remove specific sequences of DNA.

1972 – Scientists produce recombinant DNA by joining DNA from different species and inserting this into a 'host' cell.

1973 – The first animal gene is cloned by joining a frog gene to bacterial DNA.

1976 – The first genetic engineering (biotechnology) company, Genentech, is started.

1987 – Scientists discover that artificial chromosomes made from yeast can carry large fragments of human DNA.

1990 – The Human Genome Project is launched; it is planned to take 15 years.

1994 – The US Food and Drug Administration approves the sale of the first GM food (a tomato).

1996 – A complete gene map of the lab mouse is produced.

2003 – The Human Genome Project is completed.

2005 – Britain's House of Lords rules that it is legal for a couple to screen embryos in order to select a match for an older child with a genetic disease.

2005 – British scientists successfully clone human embryos as a possible source of gene therapy and other treatments.

2005-2006 – Denmark becomes the first European country to tax farmers who grow GM crops.

2007-2008 – Human-animal embryos approved for research.

2008 – Scientists discuss the possibility of regenerating extinct species like the mammoth from DNA found in ancient fossils.

ORGANISATIONS AND GLOSSARY

Council for Responsible Genetics
5 Upland Road
Suite 3 Cambridge
MA 02140
USA
Tel: +1 617 868 0870
Fax: +1 617 491 5344
Email: crg@gene-watch.org
Website: www.gene-watch.org

DEFRA (Department for Environment,
Food & Rural Affairs)
Information Resource Centre
Lower Ground Floor
Ergon House
c/o Nobel House
17 Smith Square
London SW1P 3JR
Tel: 08459 33 55 77
Fax: +44 (0) 20 7238 6609
Email: helpline@defra.gsi.gov.uk
Website: www.defra.gov.uk

Food Standards Agency
Tel: +44 (0) 20 7276 8568
Email: adekunle.adeoye@foodstandards.
gsi.gov.uk
Website: www.food.gov.uk

Gene Watch UK
The Mill House
Manchester Road

Tideswell, Buxton
Derbyshire SK17 8LN
Tel: +44 (0) 1298 871898
Fax: +44 (0) 1298 972531
Email: mail@genewatch.org
Website: www/genewatch.org

Monsanto
Monsanto UK Ltd
The Maris Centre
45 Hauxton Road
Trumpington
Cambridge CB2 2LQ
Tel: +44 (0) 1223 849 200
Fax: +44 (0) 12223 845 514
Website: www.monsanto.co.uk

Soil Association
Bristol House
40–56 Victoria Street
Bristol BS1 6BY
Tel: +44 (0) 117 314 5000
Fax: +44 (0) 117 314 5001
Email: info@soilassociation.org
Website: www.soilassociation.org

Biotechnology Australia
GPO Box 9839
Canberra ACT
Australia 2601
Email: gtis-australia@unimelb.edu.au
Website: www.biotechnology.gov.au

Clone – Any living organism that is genetically identical to another organism. Identical twins are naturally occurring clones.

Cloning – The process of producing a genetically identical copy of another cell or organism.

Embryo – An egg which has been fertilised and is beginning to develop by dividing into new cells.

Foetus – An embryo that is developing in the womb.

Gene – A short length of DNA on a chromosome that instructs the cell to produce a particular protein. This then determines features such as eye colour.

Genetic modification (GM) – The introduction of new genetic material into an organism or cell.

Genetic screening or testing – Examining adults, foetuses or embryos for genetic defects.

Gene therapy – Introducing 'normal' genes into an animal or human to replace faulty genes.

Genome – The sequence of 'bases' on DNA making up the entire genetic code of an organism.

IVF (*In Vitro* Fertilisation) – The fertilisation of eggs outside the womb.

Recombinant DNA – DNA that has been genetically modified.

Reproductive cloning – Producing cloned embryos to obtain an exact copy.

Selective breeding – Improving a required feature by inbreeding.

Stem cells – 'Undifferentiated' cells that have not yet developed into a particular kind of tissue.

Therapeutic cloning – Producing cloned embryos so that stem cells can be extracted and used for gene therapy and other purposes.

INDEX

48

Photo Credits:
Abbreviations: l-left, r-right, b-bottom, t-top, c-centre, m-middle. Front cover – b – Corbis, mr – www.istockphoto.com, ml – www.istockphoto.com / Andrei Tchernov, mc – www.istockphoto.com / Mark Evans. 6mr – A. Barrington Brown / Science Photo Library, 8t – Simon Hoyle, School of Chemistry, University of Bristol, 18t – © Balthazar Serreau / Friends of the Earth, 20mr, 38ml – Brand X Pictures, 37tr – Comstock, 13br, 24b, 31ml, 42br – Corbis, 21tl, 42mr, 44tr – Corel, 30tl – Cystic Fibrosis Trust, 5tl – Dan Mott, 44m – Digital Vision, 42tr – Flat Earth, 19b – John Foxx Images, 4tr, 43ml – Image 100, 1m, 20tl – Image Source, 4br – Peter Menzel / Science Photo Library, 8b-9b – Photodisc, 9tr – Stockbyte, 27tr – US Dept of Energy, Genome Programs, http://doegenomes.org, 2b-3b, 23bl – U.S. Navy, 39br – Wesley Bocxe / Science Photo Library, 2bl, 31bl – World Health Organisation / P. Virot, 1l, 1r, 3tr, 10mr, 10bl, 11mr, 12bl, 13tl, 14mr, 15tr, 16bl, 16tr, 17b, 21mr, 22ml, 25ml, 25tr, 26br, 26ml, 27ml, 28bl, 29tl, 29b, 30b-31b, 32tr, 32ml, 33bl, 34br, 35br, 35tr, 36bl, 36tr, 37bl, 39tl, 40t-41t, 41br, 43bl, 45mr, 45bl – www.istockphoto.com